Little Book of Wisdom

101 WORDS OF

Copyright © 1993, 1997
Brownlow Publishing Company, Inc.
6309 Airport Freeway
Fort Worth, Texas 76117

ISBN: 1-57051-204-3

Printed in USA

Blessed is the man who listens to me,

watching daily at my doors,

waiting at my doorway.

For whoever finds me finds life.

PROVERBS 8:34,35

· Words of Wisdom #101 ·

There are two ways of being rich.
One is to have all you want,
the other is to be satisfied
with what you have.

PROVERB

Easelettes

A delightful miniature product that will be a big addition to any home or office because of its small size. Containing 101 encouraging quotations, each Easelette will make a perfect gift or a great way to add a stimulating thought to your own day.

· Words of Wisdom #100 ·

I asked God for all things so I could enjoy life. He gave me life so I could enjoy all things.

Easelettes

As My Garden Grows · Dear Daughter
Dear Teacher · From Heart to Heart
From the Heart of a Friend · Heaven In Our Hearts
Home Is Where You Hang Your Memories
Little Bits of Wisdom · On Wings of Angels
Song of the Thrush · Tea Time Friends
Thoughts for My Secret Pal
When Angels Come Near · Words of Friendship

Joy is the most infallible sign
of the presence of God.

The great acts of love
are done by those who
are habitually performing
small acts of kindness.

If you haven't all the things you want,
be grateful for the things you don't have
that you wouldn't want.

Words of Wisdom #2

He has achieved success
who has lived well, laughed often,
and loved much.

BESSIE ANDERSON STANLEY

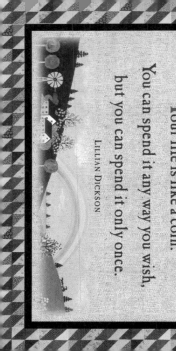

· Words of Wisdom #97 ·

Your life is like a coin.
You can spend it any way you wish,
but you can spend it only once.

LILLIAN DICKSON

· Words of Wisdom #3 ·

If you laugh a lot,
when you get older your wrinkles
will be in the right places.

The Lord is my shepherd,
I shall not be in want.

Psalm 23:1

· Words of Wisdom #4 ·

We have committed the Golden Rule
to memory, let us now commit it to life.

· Words of Wisdom #96 ·

Worry does not empty
tomorrow of its sorrow;
it empties today
of its strength.

CORRIE TEN BOOM

· Words of Wisdom #5 ·

Better keep yourself clean and bright; you are the window through which you must see the world.

G. B. SHAW

· Words of Wisdom #95 ·

The world is full of cactus,
but we don't have to sit on it.

WILL FOLEY

Heaven will be inherited by every man

who has heaven in his soul.

H. W. BEECHER

· Words of Wisdom #94 ·

Too many folks go through life
running from something
that isn't after them.

ANONYMOUS

· Words of Wisdom #7 ·

Our incomes are like shoes:
if too small, they pinch;
if too large, we stumble.

Strength is born in the deep silence of long-suffering hearts; not amid joy.

FELICIA HEMANS

For the Lord gives wisdom,
and from his mouth come
knowledge and understanding.

PROVERBS 2:6

Words of Wisdom #92

Everybody thinks of changing humanity and nobody thinks of changing himself.

LEO TOLSTOY

Words of Wisdom #8

It wasn't raining when Noah built the ark.

HOWARD RUFF

·Words of Wisdom #91·

Our Father refreshes us on the journey with some pleasant inns, but will not encourage us to mistake them for home.

C. S. LEWIS

· Words of Wisdom #9 ·

Learn from the mistakes of others.

You can't live long enough

to make them all yourself.

— Martin Vanbee

· Words of Wisdom #90 ·

It is not sufficient to have great qualities; we must be able to make proper use of them.

FRANÇOIS DE LA ROCHEFOUCAULD

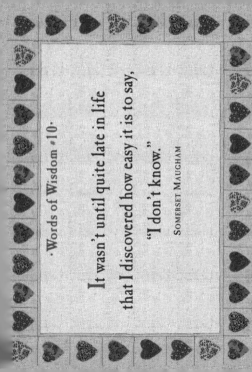

· Words of Wisdom #10·

It wasn't until quite late in life
that I discovered how easy it is to say,
"I don't know."

SOMERSET MAUGHAM

A wise man's heart guides his mouth,
and his lips promote instruction.

PROVERBS 16:23

· Words of Wisdom #11 ·

We make a living by what we get.

We make a life by what we give.

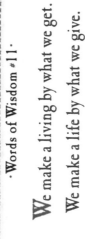

· Words of Wisdom #89 ·

It is no disgrace to be poor,
but it is mighty inconvenient.

MYRTLE MACELROY

The ideal marriage is not one
in which two people marry to be happy,
but to make each other happy.

ROY L. SMITH

· Words of Wisdom #88 ·

Some lives, like evening primroses,
blossom most beautifully
in the evening of life.

C. E. COWMAN

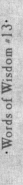

·Words of Wisdom #13·

The only things worth learning
are the things you learn
after you know it all.

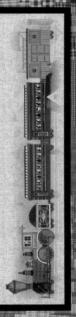

· Words of Wisdom #87 ·

Be strong! Be courageous!
Do not be afraid of them!
For the Lord your God will be with you.
He will neither fail you nor forsake you.

DEUTERONOMY 31:6

· Words of Wisdom #14 ·

For every minute
you are angry,
you lose sixty seconds
of happiness.

We are always getting ready to live,
but never living.

EMERSON

The fear of the Lord is the beginning of wisdom; all who follow his precepts have good understanding.

PSALM 111:10

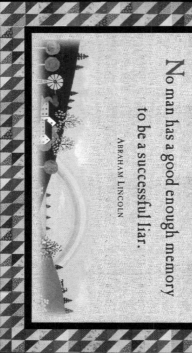

· Words of Wisdom #85 ·

No man has a good enough memory
to be a successful liar.

ABRAHAM LINCOLN

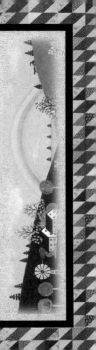

· Words of Wisdom #15 ·

Happiness is like a potato salad—when shared with others, it's a picnic.

· Words of Wisdom #84 ·

We are all here for a spell,
get all the good laughs you can.

WILL ROGERS

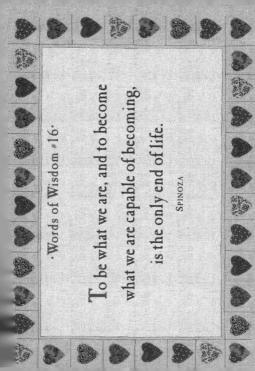

· Words of Wisdom #16 ·

To be what we are, and to become
what we are capable of becoming,
is the only end of life.

SPINOZA

· Words of Wisdom #83 ·

If you ever find happiness
by hunting for it, you will find it,
as the old woman did her lost spectacles,
safe on her own nose all the time.

JOSH BILLINGS

· Words of Wisdom #17 ·

One of the hardest decisions in life
is when to start middle age.

Rebuke a wise man and he will love you. Instruct a wise man and he will be wiser still.

PROVERBS 9:8, 9

· Words of Wisdom #18 ·

No God, no peace.

Know God, know peace.

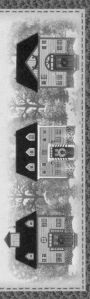

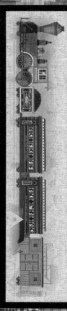

· Words of Wisdom #82 ·

Let us be at least as generous in judging
others as we are in judging ourselves.

O. S. MARDEN

· Words of Wisdom #19 ·

Grief can take care of itself;
but to get the full value of joy you must
have somebody to divide it with.

MARK TWAIN

We miss the really great
joys of life scrambling
for bargain-counter happiness.

Roy L. Smith

Failure is the

opportunity to begin again

more intelligently.

I believe the first test of a truly
great man is his humility.

JOHN RUSKIN

Words of Wisdom #21

Your character is what you have left
when you've lost everything you can lose.

· Words of Wisdom #79·

I will listen to anyone's convictions,
but pray keep your doubts to yourself;
I have plenty of my own.

GOETHE

For wisdom is more precious than rubies, and nothing you desire can compare with her.

PROVERBS 8:11

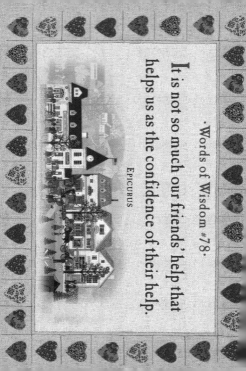

· Words of Wisdom #78 ·

It is not so much our friends' help that helps us as the confidence of their help.

EPICURUS

· Words of Wisdom #22 ·

Don't bother to give God instructions;
just report for duty.

CORRIE TEN BOOM

· Words of Wisdom #77 ·

I shall allow no man to belittle
my soul by making me hate him.

BOOKER T. WASHINGTON

Much happiness is overlooked because it doesn't cost anything.

OSCAR WILDE

Y ou may not realize it when it happens, but a kick in the teeth may be the best thing in the world for you.

WALT DISNEY

He is a wise man who does not grieve for the things which he has not, but rejoices for those which he has.

EPICTETUS

If any of you lacks wisdom,
he should ask God,
who gives generously to all.

JAMES 1:5

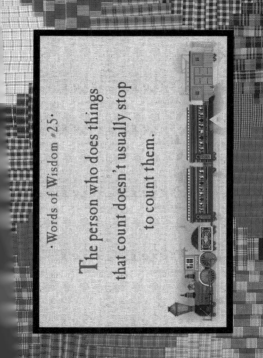

· Words of Wisdom #25 ·

The person who does things
that count doesn't usually stop
to count them.

·Words of Wisdom #75·

Sometimes one pays most
for the things one gets
for nothing.

ALBERT EINSTEIN

· Words of Wisdom #26 ·

We can be knowledgeable with other men's knowledge, but we cannot be wise with other men's wisdom.

MICHEL EYQUEM DE MONTAIGNE

Every man can tell how many
goats or sheep he possesses,
but not how many friends.

CICERO

For God so loved the world that he gave his one and only Son, that whoever believes in him shall not perish but have eternal life.

JOHN 3:16

· Words of Wisdom #73 ·

As sure as God ever puts
His children into the furnace,
He will be in the furnace with them.

CHARLES H. SPURGEON

· Words of Wisdom #27 ·

No person was ever honored
for what he received. Honor has been
the reward for what he gave.

CALVIN COOLIDGE

· Words of Wisdom #72 ·

He that is good for making excuses
is seldom good for anything else.

BEN FRANKLIN

· Words of Wisdom #28·

Commit to the Lord whatever you do,
and your plans will succeed.

PROVERBS 16:3

· Words of Wisdom #71 ·

We may elevate ourselves
but we should never reach so high
that we would ever forget those
who helped us get there.

WILL ROGERS

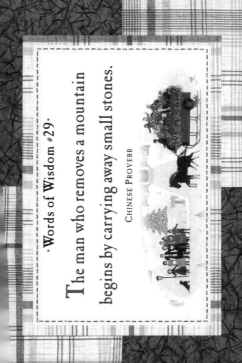

· Words of Wisdom #29·

The man who removes a mountain
begins by carrying away small stones.

CHINESE PROVERB

A man can hardly be said
to have made a fortune if he
does not know how to enjoy it.

VAUVENARGUES

· Words of Wisdom #30 ·

In the old days a fool and his money were

soon parted. Now it happens to everyone.

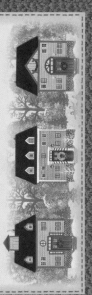

Better do a good deed near at home
than go far away to burn incense.

CHINESE PROVERB

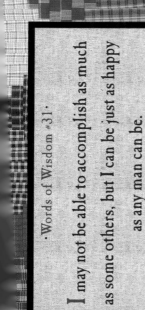

· Words of Wisdom #31 ·

I may not be able to accomplish as much as some others, but I can be just as happy as any man can be.

CHARLES ALLEN

He who walks
with the wise grows wise,
but a companion of fools
suffers harm.

PROVERBS 13:20

Let me tell thee,
time is a very precious gift of God;
so precious that it's only
given to us moment by moment.

AMELIA BARR

· Words of Wisdom #68 ·

Life is not so short but that there is always time for courtesy.

EMERSON

· Words of Wisdom #33 ·

Life is like an onion;
you peel off one layer at a time
and sometimes you weep.

CARL SANDBURG

· Words of Wisdom #67 ·

Enjoy your life without
comparing it with that of others.

CONDORCET

Blessed is the man who finds wisdom, the man who gains understanding.

PROVERBS 3:13

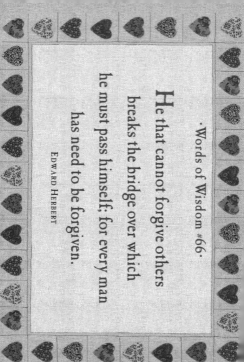

· Words of Wisdom #66 ·

He that cannot forgive others
breaks the bridge over which
he must pass himself; for every man
has need to be forgiven.

EDWARD HERBERT

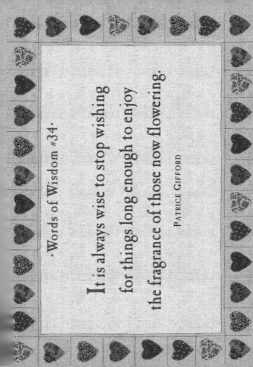

· Words of Wisdom #34·

It is always wise to stop wishing

for things long enough to enjoy

the fragrance of those now flowering.

PATRICE GIFFORD

Circumstances do not make the man; they only reveal him to himself.

JAMES ALLEN

· Words of Wisdom #35 ·

The future is that time
when you'll wish you'd done
what you aren't doing now.

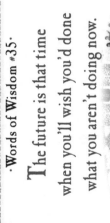

We are apt to forget that children watch examples better than they listen to preaching.

Roy L. Smith

· Words of Wisdom #36 ·

God will not look you over for medals,
degrees or diplomas but for scars.

HUBBARD

· Words of Wisdom #63 ·

He who could foresee affairs
three days in advance would be rich
for thousands of years.

FROM THE CHINESE

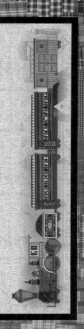

· Words of Wisdom #37 ·

You will never "find" time for anything. If you want time you must make it.

CHARLES BUXTON

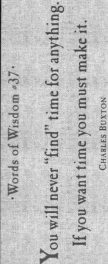

The person who says
"it can't be done"
is liable to be interrupted
by someone doing it.

Be a life long or short,
its completeness depends
on what it was lived for.

DAVID STARR JORDAN

The earth is the Lord's,
and everything in it, the world,
and all who live in it.

PSALM 24:1

Words of Wisdom #39

Ninety percent of the friction of daily life is caused by the wrong tone of voice.

· Words of Wisdom #61 ·

A good book contains more
real wealth than a good bank.

ROY L. SMITH

· Words of Wisdom #40 ·

Nothing will ever be attempted
if all possible objections
must be first overcome.

SAMUEL JOHNSON

· Words of Wisdom #60 ·

The great tragedy of life is not
unanswered prayer, but unoffered prayer.

PHILIP MELANCHTHON

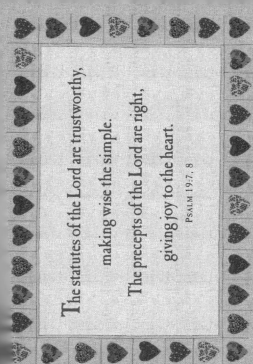

The statutes of the Lord are trustworthy,

making wise the simple.

The precepts of the Lord are right,

giving joy to the heart.

PSALM 19:7, 8

· Words of Wisdom #59 ·

Happiness grows at our own
firesides, and is not to be picked
in strangers' gardens.

DOUGLAS JERROLD

· Words of Wisdom #41 ·

My great concern is not whether God is on our side, my great concern is to be on God's side.

ABRAHAM LINCOLN

Some people are making
such thorough preparations for
a rainy day that they aren't enjoying
today's sunshine.

· Words of Wisdom #42 ·

Happiness is a thing to be practiced,
like the violin.

JOHN LUBBOCK

· Words of Wisdom #57 ·

If you are patient in one moment
of anger, you will escape
a hundred days of sorrow.

CHINESE PROVERB

· Words of Wisdom #43 ·

And my God will meet
all your needs according to his
glorious riches in Christ Jesus.

PHILIPPIANS 4:19

· Words of Wisdom #56 ·

A large part of good manners
is to know when to pretend
that what's happening isn't happening.

Good character, like good soup,

is made at home.

People who want milk
should not seat themselves on a stool
in the middle of a field in hope
that a cow will back up to them.

ELBERT HUBBARD

· Words of Wisdom #45 ·

If you sow thorns,
you will not reap roses.

Buy the truth and do not sell it;
get widsom, discipline
and understanding.

PROVERBS 23:23

· Words of Wisdom #46 ·

An oxcart is as useless to a man
as a rocket ship if he does not know
where he wants to go.

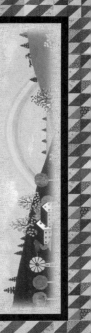

·Words of Wisdom #54·

Those who can't forget are worse off than those who can't remember.

· Words of Wisdom #47 ·

Too many people are ready to carry the
stool when the piano needs to be moved.

·Words of Wisdom #53·

Money is a wonderful thing,
but it is possible to pay
too high a price for it.

Wisdom is supreme; therefore get wisdom. Though it cost all you have, get understanding.

PROVERBS 4:7

If there be any truer measure
of a man than by what he does,
it must be by what he gives.

ROBERT SOUTH

· Words of Wisdom #48 ·

Before a man can wake up
and find himself famous, he has to
wake up and find himself.

· Words of Wisdom #51 ·

I am not afraid of tomorrow,
for I have seen yesterday and I love today.

WILLIAM ALLEN WHITE

· Words of Wisdom #49 ·

Temper merely shows lack of control and places you temporarily in the ranks of lunatics and fools.

WILLIAM NICKERSON

We are all in the same boat
in a stormy sea, and we owe each other
a terrible loyalty.

G. K. CHESTERTON

Be careful, then,
how you live—not as unwise
but as wise, making the most
of every opportunity.

EPHESIANS 5:15, 16

When pride comes,
then comes disgrace,
but with humility comes wisdom.

PROVERBS 11:2